PLEASE DON'T JUST DO WHAT I TELL YOU!
DO WHAT NEEDS TO BE DONE

PLEASE
DON'T JUST
DO WHAT
I TELL YOU!*

*DO WHAT NEEDS TO BE DONE
Every Employee's Guide to Making Work More Rewarding

BOB NELSON, PH.D.

HYPERION
NEW YORK

Library of Congress Cataloging-in-Publication Data

Nelson, Bob.
    Please don't just do what I tell you, do what needs to be
done : every employee's guide to making work more
rewarding / by Bob Nelson
        p.   cm.
    ISBN 0-7868-6729-9
    1. Employee empowerment.   2. Labor productivity.
3. Employee motivation.   I. Title.
    HD50.5 .N45   2001
    650.1--dc21   2001039175

FIRST EDITION

10 9 8 7 6 5 4 3 2 1

Foreword

Bob Nelson and I have been colleagues and friends for more than fifteen years. This book, *Please Don't Just Do What I Tell You! Do What Needs to Be Done*, has a wonderful history. Bob and I talked for some time about possibly writing a book together around *Message to Garcia*, that classic fable about the importance of employees doing what they are told to do. Now, more than a decade later, Bob has appropriately repositioned that message to one that is more in tune with the times.

Why? The old deal is over at work. Loyalty used to get you job security. When I graduated from Cornell, a friend of mine got a job at AT&T. He called home and his mother cried. She said, "You are set for life." Today, regardless of where you work, nobody is set for life. With the amount of change facing every organization today, all bets are off for the future.

If the old deal is off, what is the new deal? In talking to people around the world, I have asked, "If you can't get job security at work, what do you want?" They tell me they want two things: honesty and opportunity. First, today's employees want the straight story—they don't want to be lied to. "Don't tell us you are not going to lay people off and then go ahead and do so six months later." Second, today's employees want opportunity: opportunity to learn, to build knowledge, and to develop their skills. People know that their best job security is to increase their marketability and the value they have to offer where they work.

Tom Peters is talking all the time now about "Brand You." Everyone soon will have their own portfolio describing the opportunities they have had and the skills they bring to the party. The best way for people to learn today is to have opportunities to take initiative. People have to have a chance to make mistakes and to learn from those mistakes. And they have to have the strategies and techniques to make a difference at work. That's what this book is all about. Bob shows that we each can create our own opportunity, regardless of where we work or the job we do.

Bob's message is also timely in that the great organizations that are beating the competition today are those that are customer-focused. There's nothing that drives a customer crazy quicker than to have a front-line employee quack like a duck and say: "I'm sorry, it's our policy," or "I just work here," or "Do you want to talk to my supervisor?" Enlightened customers today want to deal with somebody who has the power to make decisions. That's what beats the competition, and that's what keeps your workforce motivated.

The best organizations are finding that the best service comes from employees who are given a chance to have an impact in their jobs. Again, Bob's book shows us that for every position, at any level, employees are closer than anyone else to the problems and opportunities of their own jobs, and thus better able to make a difference with their customers, colleagues, and even their managers.

Read *Please Don't Just Do What I Tell You! Do What Needs to Be Done* and tell everyone you know about it! It will really help you create opportunities for yourself and those with whom you work to make a difference. My guess is that your boss will like it too. Good on you all!

Ken Blanchard, Ph.D.
Co-author, *The One Minute Manager*

Preface

This book has a simple premise: You never need permission to do great work. Wherever you work, whomever you work for, management expects that you will *always* use your own best judgment and effort to do what needs to be done for the organization to be successful.

I call this *The Ultimate Expectation*. It's a message that every employee needs to hear, but one that few employers explicitly state.

Although it may sound strange, every employer today is looking to hire essentially the same person: someone who takes initiative. Of course, specific employers' needs are as varied as the skills and abilities of the workers they hire; but at the core, it's the same individual they seek. The person who—regardless of his or her background, training, or abilities—can be dropped into a work situation and take independent action is worth his or her weight in gold.

Being able to fulfill The Ultimate Expectation is a virtue every worker possesses, but few seem to demonstrate. To do what needs to be done without being told is the hallmark of professional excellence.

To serve a customer, solve a problem, assist a co-worker, make a money-saving suggestion, develop an idea, or improve a process are actions that are needed from all employees every day, indeed, every moment they are employed.

In fact, I know of no company today that can survive with employees doing only what they are told to do. The competitive environment, the amount of change, and the speed of business today in most markets is too intense for employees to act otherwise. An organization that expects employees to do only what they are told is on a slippery slope to being out of business in just a matter of time.

Compare your company with any of its competitors. More likely than not, you have similar products and services, technology and channels of distribution, marketing strategies, and more.

What makes one company a success while another struggles to survive? It's the people—and the daily initiative, energy, and commitment these people bring to their work, without waiting to be told what to do.

The days of "superiors" and "subordinates" are long past. Work today is a partnership, and everyone's in it together. The nature of work—of business itself—is changing too quickly for employees to wait for direction. They must jump in with both feet.

Employees know best how to do their own jobs better. They are most familiar with the problems that arise in their jobs, as well as the needs of the customers they serve. They see and experience firsthand what most upper managers can only infer from reports. For employees at all levels to be engaged and thinking about how to do their jobs better allows the organization to be more responsive to its customers—and more competitive in achieving its goals.

We are fast moving toward being a nation of self-managed employees, in which every person needs to understand the importance of his or her individual contribution to the organization's mission and purpose, and strive to take initiative to have a greater impact on the job, department, and organization.

Along the way, your work will become more exciting, you will see the impact of your actions, and you will learn, grow, and develop in your position. You'll gain a reputation as someone who "makes things happen" and be better able to take on larger and more significant responsibilities and reap the rewards for doing so.

This book is intended to be a starting point for further discussion. It represents an attitude and philosophy whose time has come, an attitude that can benefit every member of the organization—as well as the organization as a whole.

Bob Nelson
San Diego, California
Spring 2001

Contents

Part One

INTRODUCTION: A MESSAGE WHOSE TIME HAS COME

Like many people, I held some interesting jobs as a teenager and in college. I had a job assembling bicycles (I was fired). I sold dictionaries door-to-door. I once spent a summer collecting unpaid tickets for a beauty pageant, ordered from sweet-talking contestants by middle-aged men who never intended to actually go. I've worked as a math tutor, a bookstore receiving clerk, a 7-Eleven cashier, and a summer camp Boy Scout counselor. I've done yard work and maintenance work for room and board to help get through college.

Most of these jobs were mundane to the point of being boring. They seemed to me at the time to have in common only the fact that they were each menial, minimum-wage jobs.

I learned later that I was wrong. Each of these jobs offered valuable lessons and opportunities that I ignored—lessons I've since learned could be obtained in *any* job, at *any* level!

Take, for example, my job at 7-Eleven. I felt I was a good employee. I did what I was told to do and what I felt was expected in my job, which seemed to consist primarily of standing behind the cash register, waiting to ring up customer purchases.

One day, however, I was standing behind the cash register talking with another employee when the regional manager walked in the door. He glanced around the store for a moment, then motioned for me to come with him down one of the aisles. Without saying a word, he started to front merchandise, that is, to move up inventory to replace products that had been purchased.

He then walked to the food preparation area, wiped down the counter, and emptied a full trash receptacle.

I observed all of this with curiosity, and it slowly dawned on me that he expected me to do all the things he was doing! This came as a complete surprise to me, not because any of the tasks he was doing was new (I had done them all before; for example, I would mop the floor and empty the trash every day before my shift was done), but because the assumption was that I needed to be doing these tasks *all the time*!

Well, nobody had ever explicitly told me this before! And even now it was unstated.

In that unspoken moment, I learned

a lesson about the world of work that would serve me for the rest of my life—a lesson that not only made me a better employee, but also allowed me to get more out of every job and work experience from that moment forward.

The lesson was that I needed to be responsible for my own work. I needed to accept a higher level of ownership for my job in which I held myself personally accountable for my actions. In short, I needed to focus on what needed to be done and not wait to be told what to do.

Once I grasped this lesson, jobs I had found mundane became much more fun and exciting to me. The more I focused on what I could do in the job, the more I was able to learn and accomplish.

I left the 7-Eleven job to go to college, but I took something from that experience that shaped my life and career in a profound way. I went from being a bystander to taking charge of my work experiences. Class projects became more interesting, part-time jobs and internships became opportunities to explore entire professions, and entry-level positions became portals for unprecedented opportunity and growth.

As I advanced to higher positions as a manager and executive, I always tried to find opportunities to do what needed to be done. In fact, in every job, at every level, I saw chances to excel and make a difference—not just for my employer, but for myself as well.

I came to the conclusion that every employee in every job needs to hear and believe this fundamental message: You can start to make a difference with your life today, in the job you currently hold, not the ideal job you hope you might hold someday in the distant future.

In the following pages, you'll gain further insight into how to take charge of your job, your career, and your life.

Our journey starts with an imaginary letter to new employees I call "The Ultimate Expectation."

Part Two

THE ULTIMATE EXPECTATION: DO WHAT NEEDS TO BE DONE

Dear Employee:

You've been hired to handle some pressing needs we have. If we could have gotten by in not hiring you, we would have. But we've determined that we needed someone with your skills and experience and that you were the best person to help us with our needs. We have offered you the position and you've accepted. Thanks!

During the course of your employment, you will be asked to do many things: general responsibilities, specific assignments, group and individual projects. You will have many chances to excel and to confirm that we made a good choice in hiring you.

However, there is one foremost responsibility that may never be specifically requested of you but that you need to always keep in mind through the duration of your employment. This is The Ultimate Expectation, and it is as follows:

ALWAYS DO WHAT MOST NEEDS TO BE DONE WITHOUT WAITING TO BE ASKED.

We've hired you to do a job, yes, but more important, we've hired you to think, use your judgment and act in the best interests of the organization at all times.

If we never say this again, don't take it as an indication that it's no longer important or that we've changed our priorities. We are likely to get caught up in the daily press of business, the never-ending changes of the operation, and the ongoing rush of activities. Our day-to-day practices may make it look like this principle no longer applies. Don't be deceived by this.

Please don't ever forget The Ultimate Expectation. Strive to have it always be a guiding principle in your employment with us, a philosophy that is always with you, one that is constantly driving your thoughts and actions.

As long as you are employed with us, you have our permission to act in our mutual best interests.

If at any time you do not feel we are doing the right thing—the thing you most believe would help us all—please say so. You have our permission to speak up when necessary to state what is unstated, to make a suggestion, or to question an action or decision.

This doesn't mean we will always agree with you, nor that we will necessarily change what we are doing; but we always want to hear what you most believe would help us better achieve our goals and purpose and to create a mutually successful experience in the process.

You will need to seek to understand how (and why) things are done the way they are done before you seek to change existing work processes. Try to work with the systems that are in place first, but tell us if you think those systems need to be changed.

Discuss what is presented here with me and others in the organization so that we might all become better at applying The Ultimate Expectation.

Sincerely,

Your Manager

P.S.: Like much sound advice, The Ultimate Expectation seems like common sense. Don't confuse what sounds simple with what is easy to do. Take this message to heart and become skilled at applying it to your own job and circumstances. Once you learn The Ultimate Expectation, you must apply it on a daily basis to your work. Accepting this challenge is paramount to your success with us, in your career, and in your life.

Part Three

SIMPLE STRATEGIES AND TECHNIQUES: WAYS TO GET STARTED NOW

Think—What Needs to Be Done?

All actions of consequence start with a thought, with someone thinking he or she can do something different from and better than what is currently being done. The following are some of the lessons, strategies, tips, and techniques I've learned in taking initiative. Use them to trigger your own thinking to come up with ideas for specific application in your current position.

Whenever possible, look for ways to make your job more difficult. Take on work, volunteer to help others, and ask to be on projects or teams created to address pressing problems.

Sure, in the short run, this strategy may make you frazzled, but in the long run, it will show that you are a person capable and eager to take on challenges—and your worth to the organization will rise accordingly.

Take, for example, Sharon Leahy, an executive assistant at Tri-United Companies, a real estate company located in Skokie, Illinois. She systematically took on responsibilities to help her manager, and as she did so, her job was expanded to include the duties of an office manager. She is now vice president of the company. Leahy reports: "When the boss is away, I am completely in charge of the entire operation." Moshe Menora, owner of Tri-United, loves it: "Any boss is looking for somebody who is assertive to the point where he or she can command without being asked to command and assist without being asked to assist."

Likewise, Emily Rodriguez, an employee at Esprit De Corp, steadily increased her corporate responsibilities by simply advocating new ways of using logistics as a service and marketing tool, ranging from overseas cargo consolidations to prepaid freight programs. Now she's director of transportation for the San Francisco–based firm.

By stretching yourself in your job, you not only can achieve more, but, along the way, you will also learn more, making it easier to leverage your past successes into future opportunities.

Strive to understand your job, to respond to your manager's needs, and to be proactive in expanding your responsibilities.

Most actions start with a thought, and you can easily control what you think about. At work, try to think about how things could be improved.

Start small. Think how you might better organize your work, for example. Come in a little early to plan your day before everyone is in the office. When asked a question, try to determine the question behind the question. Make a point of periodically asking your manager if there is anything else you can help him or her with. Look for the unspoken needs of those around you that you can assist with, to help make their jobs a little easier.

When I was a receiving clerk for a bookstore, I found the job was more fun if I made suggestions. It got me thinking in new ways about what I was doing; time passed more quickly; and every now and then, an idea of mine would get other people interested and talking—and their excitement fed my own.

Don't assume there is only one correct way to do a given task. Don't assume the way things have always been done is the best way to continue doing them. Don't assume that no one cares if things are done better.

Make at least two suggestions a week in your job. Suggest how things could be improved, how money could be saved, or how processes could be streamlined. Focus first on your own job, and then, as you gain skill, confidence, and respect, make suggestions in your department, and then in the overall company.

Constantly be on the lookout for ways to save the company money, and treat company funds as if they were your own.

Every organization is interested in ways to accomplish more and save money in the process. Be on the lookout for cost-saving ideas that will make you more valuable to your employer.

A shipping clerk at Boardroom, Inc., a newsletter and book publisher based in Greenwich, Connecticut, suggested the company might consider trimming the paper size of one of its books when it was next reprinted so that, when shipped, it would fall under a lower postal rate.

Trim they did, and in the first year alone, they saved $500,000 in postage costs! Marty Edelston, the chairman of the firm, says: "I'd been working in mail order for twenty-three years and I didn't even know there was a fourth-class postal rate—but the person shipping books every day did!"

The person who performs a task is in the best position to see how to do it better, and save money in the process. This same person typically knows how the organization could save money in other ways as well, or how things could be done more efficiently throughout the company.

Get a second bid on contracted work and purchases. Explore the cost benefits to leasing versus buying equipment. Suggest the department have a potluck celebration instead of purchasing lunch for everyone. See if any in-house employees might be interested in work being contracted outside the company. Ask for volunteers instead of scheduling overtime. Consider interns for handling some project work. The possibilities for being thrifty are endless.

There's never such a thing as a silly question, even if it sounds silly at the time. The question you ask may have never been asked before; or if it was, perhaps the timing has changed and the idea is now more viable.

One day, Elaine Crawford, a secretary at Johnsonville Foods, a sausage wholesaler in Sheboygan Falls, Wisconsin, asked her boss: "Is there any reason why we don't sell our product directly to consumers?"

Her boss, Ralph Stayer, said she should look into that idea, and soon Elaine was personally managing a multimillion-dollar division in direct sales to consumers.

Once in a management meeting when the group was discussing terminating an employee, I asked, "Has the person ever been told that he could lose his job if he did not improve?"

It turned out that he had never been told that; and by setting clearer expectations and potential consequences, the company quite likely avoided a lawsuit.

Especially in changing times, the way things have always been done in the past may not be the best way to continue doing them in the future; and there's no better way to find out than to ask.

Ask questions about why things are done as they are. Ask what happens before the work gets to you and where it goes after you are done. Ask your customers if they value the features or services that are being provided—and if they are willing to pay more for those benefits. Ask others if they could make a change in how things were done, what would it be? Ask your manager how you could be a better employee.

Every need is an opportunity. Learn to look at your customers' needs and ask how you might satisfy those needs. Learn to look at your organization's needs with an eye for how those needs might be creatively solved.

An employee at Kacey's Fine Furniture in Denver, Colorado, was concerned that the hours that the store was open prevented many customers who worked during the day from shopping there. So she suggested that the store hours be changed. Her plan was implemented, and as a result, sales increased 15 percent.

Shop workers at Atlanta's Georgia-Pacific Corporation, the leading manufacturer and distributor of building products in the United States, took a by-product of their operation—sawdust from their lumber mill—and turned it into a revenue source by selling it to nurseries to be used for mulch. By thinking about who might need or could use their by-product, they were able to create a new market for their company.

I worked with an organization that

had limited parking for employees. Employees wanted the organization to build a parking structure even though the cost was in the millions of dollars. Management responded that money was not available in the budget.

No one in this organization ever looked at other ways the parking need could be resolved, such as through telecommuting, staggered shifts, job sharing, ride sharing, shuttle services, incentivized long-distance parking, and so forth. The need could have easily been addressed through creatively exploring opportunities and looking at the need from different perspectives.

For each need you encounter, try to identify three ways the need could be addressed and who might benefit from the situation. Ask "what if" questions to explore what could be done to meet customer needs.

CAUTION

DON'T BE A COMPLAINER

Many employees grouse about their jobs, their managers, and even their customers, and never seem to realize that they are in part responsible for their own circumstances. They focus on the negative and feel they always get the short end of the stick. If something goes wrong, they blame management or others in the organization for not giving them adequate resources, advance warning about changes, and so on. It's like they're passive observers of their own lives.

Most organizations are filled with employees who are never satisfied with their circumstances. They wait for their managers to become enlightened and expect more from their company and others around them than they are willing to give themselves. Don't be one of these employees, and avoid employees who constantly complain—you don't want their bad habits to rub off on you.

Prepare—Do Your Homework

Very few good ideas are converted into concrete actions without some preparation along the way.

This preparation can be broad, such as learning about your industry or another area of the company or developing accounting skills, or it can be very specific, such as creating a cost-benefit analysis or a PowerPoint presentation for an idea you want to pursue.

Once you have an idea of what could be done differently, you need to prepare to implement that idea. Preparation can take many forms, from discussing the idea with co-workers, to collecting data, to researching the problem and how others have handled similar situations, both inside or outside of your organization.

The more you think through an idea, its pros and cons, costs and benefits, and steps to completion, the greater the likelihood your idea will meet with success.

☞ LEARN WHAT YOU DON'T
KNOW FIRST

Focus on learning what you don't understand at work before you try to persuade others about what you think should be done differently. Find out what they know and minimize what you don't know.

Our impulse when we first have an idea is to want to push it on those around us, expecting each person to be receptive and impressed by our insight and brilliance. But it is far better to first try to understand why things are the way they are than to blindly seek to change them. The appreciation you gain in learning why things are as they are can help you to predict objections to and concerns about changing current practices.

One corporation put together a cross-functional task force to eliminate unnecessary paperwork. The group obtained a master list of reports from the Information Services department and systematically eliminated more than 10 percent of the reports. They congratulated themselves on their success and the savings to the organization, and disbanded. But ultimately, every report that was eliminated had to be reinstated, as people complained about not having information they needed in their jobs.

When seeking change, start with those individuals who are most vested in the current way of doing things and ask their opinions about making improvements. By asking for and incorporating their feedback, you will increase the chances of obtaining their support and that your efforts will be successful.

Interview others, ask co-workers, query your clients about processes, procedures, and past history until you have a good "feel" for why things are as they are. Along the way, you'll hear and see what needs to change and be able to test those changes with those individuals who are most vested in the outcome.

In any job, you can do simple research to test your ideas and collect data to back up your recommendations. How often does a machine need repair and when should proactive maintenance be conducted? How many times does a customer ask for a certain service? How often do you perform a step in a process that could be eliminated altogether? What does it cost when a request is "rushed"?

One executive I know took over a customized product area in which nothing was going well. He spent hours interviewing the area's customers and collected seven pages of negative comments from them.

He presented his findings to the group and challenged them to come up with a key indicator that they could rally around and start to improve. The group settled on "on-time" project delivery.

They made a big deal about the very first project that was completed on time, announcing it to the rest of the organization, who for the most part scoffed and snickered. Comments like "They finally finished one on time" were heard in the hallway.

But the group kept at it and soon had five projects in a row completed on time, then seventeen, then twenty-two, and so on. All the laughing stopped, and salespeople who had sworn they would never work with the group began to contact them about potential projects.

As a result, the department went from being a problem area to being a primary asset of the organization—and a significant source of revenue. Fifteen months later, on this particular executive's last day in the department, the group had completed its 1,700th on-time project in a row!

A self-managed team of drill operators at Copeland Corporation, a refrigeration and air-conditioning manufacturer located in Sidney, Ohio, researched the viability of using a higher-quality drill bit to replace one that was causing quality problems with production. Their research showed that a drill bit that cost twice as much would last three times as long, thereby reducing damaged goods and machine downtime.

Solid data is a good foundation for systematic improvement. By monitoring the needs and practicalities of your own job, you can determine when it makes sense to initiate a needed change—and have the evidence in hand to make your request persuasive to others.

Systematically track relevant data about recurring situations: time spent, deviations, special requests, progress against goals, etc.

☞ DEVELOP OPTIONS AND A PLAN OF ACTION

The best plans consider a variety of options and advocate a course of action that best matches the circumstances of the situation.

An employee of a small company was charged with developing a plan for trade shows, something she had never done before. She interviewed the president and sales staff to see what type of trade show they felt would be best for the company to attend. Based on the available budget and time away from the office, a target number of trade shows was selected. Armed with this information, she developed criteria for size, type, and geographic location, then went online to explore possibilities.

She developed a list of possible trade shows, called for any additional information that was needed, rank-ordered the list according to the preset criteria, and presented her findings and recommendations to the staff. Once the specific trade shows were identified, she proceeded to create a master list of things to do to make the shows a success, all along communicating with everyone who had a role or vested interest in the plans.

In another example, when news spread that U.S. Airways planned to shut down its maintenance operations in Winston-Salem, North Carolina, laying off 1,300 workers in the process, employees took action. On their own initiative, they developed and presented an alternate proposal to management— one that suggested consolidating the maintenance operations from other parts of the country to their facility, thus helping the company increase efficiencies while at the same time saving their own jobs.

Look at new possibilities and combinations. Consider different ways the same goal could be achieved. Involve others in your ideas to gain their sense of ownership, support, and potential for action.

Brainstorm possibilities, develop criteria for evaluating acceptable solutions, select the best alternative, and think through the details of a plan for achieving the best solution.

You've probably heard the saying, "The devil is in the details." For years I had heard it, but I never quite understood what it meant until I became a professional speaker.

As a presenter, I learned over time that anything that could go wrong eventually did: the wrong room, the wrong date, equipment that doesn't work, no control over the temperature or lighting, missing or incorrect handouts, and on and on. I came to learn firsthand that it is precisely those details you don't double-check that are the most likely to go wrong! Now I make it a point to get to any presentation with plenty of time prior to my presentation to check over *everything*.

At Intel, management enables any employee to object to or challenge an idea or decision through a philosophy they call "intellectual honesty." Employees are encouraged to speak out against those ideas and actions they don't believe in. The process tends to make the ultimate decision or action stronger and more effective.

If you have a proposal you are putting forth to management, think through all the steps and consequences of your idea.

What resources will be needed? How long will it take? Why shouldn't the group wait for another time? Who else in the company will be affected by the resulting change? What predictable questions and objections will come up? What is most likely to go wrong?

Initially, you need to look back to prepare well, but as you near implementation, you need to look ahead to think through and anticipate problems. The better you can think through an idea, the better you can see what needs to be done to make it happen. If there are no foreseen problems or objections, you can be sure that more work is yet needed!

☞ REALIZE NO ONE CARES ABOUT YOUR IDEAS

Many employees feel a good idea will almost magically be noticed and acted upon in any organization. This rarely happens. In fact, the opposite is more likely to be true: No one will have the energy that you have for your own ideas.

You, therefore, need to be the person who creates the energy and builds support for your own ideas, talking them up, asking others for their opinions, involving them, and seeking their support.

Many years ago, John Patrick, an employee of IBM in Somers, New York, believed that the Internet would be the future of computing. He wrote an internal memo calling on all IBMers to "Get connected." In it, he identified a number of principles that would reshape the industry and made a case for his theory.

His memo got noticed, thanks to his hard work, and responses soon followed. According to Patrick, "People didn't know where I reported in the company and they didn't care."

When IBM created a 600-person division to define the company's Internet initiatives a few years later, Patrick was named its vice president and chief technology officer.

A shipping clerk in a warehouse knew his company's stated values listed "service to customers" as a priority, yet it often seemed the only time anyone in shipping heard about customers was because of a complaint: Something was missing, broken in shipping, or arrived late.

He wanted to change this but wasn't sure how. He thought it would be better if there was some way the shipping department could hear from customers who were pleased with their order and how it was packaged and shipped. When he brought this idea up to his supervisor, he was told: "We've got enough to do now, without trying to dig up more complaints."

Undeterred, he kept talking up the idea with his colleagues, and one day he noticed someone from the marketing department in the lunchroom. He sat down with this person and asked if there was any way she could make up some type of return postcard that could be included with each order shipped. The marketing person told him to send her a copy of what he wanted it to say and she would lay it out for him. The next week, he took the postcard to the shipping supervisor and asked if he could try it in all orders for a week. The response from customers and the reaction in the department were so positive that they turned it into a business-reply card that is now included with every order that is shipped.

Look around and define what needs to be done. Then ask others for help and thank them for their assistance. Make your ideas be viewed as *their* ideas.

CAUTION

DON'T PLAY GAMES AT WORK

Don't play games—gossiping, politicking, scheming—at work. Come to work to do your job and do it well. When others play games, keep focused on your own job and goals.

When you share information about others at work, remember these guiding questions: "Is it true?" "Is it kind?" "Is it necessary?"

Be known as someone positive. Doing what needs to be done includes being an advocate for those you work for and with. Don't dwell on the negative but rather be the person who is continually positive and forward-looking.

Act—Do Something Different Now

Of course, you want to have done your preparation carefully, but ultimately, the essence of initiative is taking action, that is, doing something different now.

No one will have the same energy that you have for your own ideas, so you need to be the primary advocate for turning those ideas into reality through your actions. Work within the system as best you can to get things done; and if you go outside the system, for example, to your manager's manager with an idea, examine your motives for doing so. If you believe they are in the best interests of the organization and not for personal credit or gain, this approach may well make good sense.

Even if you make a mistake, you can learn from it and try again, increasing your chances of ultimate success in the process.

We've all been in meetings that were dull and boring and going nowhere. In such situations, we tend to think, "It's not *my* meeting—I wish the leader would do something!" Like a student in a classroom, we feel it's not our place to speak out. Nothing could be further from the truth!

At one meeting I attended, I took a different approach and said: "It may just be me, but have we been over this ground before? Perhaps we should take the issue to a vote and move on."

To my surprise, many others in the meeting quickly agreed with my assessment, and everyone seemed relieved at the intervention. The meeting went from being "stuck" to suddenly having energy and momentum.

If you're in a meeting, be an active participant. If you have an idea, observation, or question, speak up! Don't expect others to know what's on your mind. Help the group in any way you can: by summarizing, keeping time, drawing out others, tracking agreed-upon items, and so forth. The more you are engaged the more you'll be able to make of your time and the time of others.

☞ VOLUNTEER FOR DIFFICULT
ASSIGNMENTS

Be quick to volunteer for tasks, projects, or additional responsibilities. When a problem arises, volunteer to help find a solution. If you can add value to a task force, join it. If you have a chance to take on additional responsibilities, always try to accept the challenge and, in the process, expand your learning and horizons. I know of employees who volunteered to create their company's website and went on to head a department as the area grew in importance to the organization.

Volunteer to take over an assignment your boss isn't very excited about: attending a meeting or making a presentation in his or her place, sorting job applications, or traveling for business, for example.

When a customer makes a request that you have never heard before, don't hide behind company policy and focus on what you *can't* do. Focus your energy instead on what you *can* do to help this person.

Listen closely, explore the situation, and suggest an alternative. Take a calculated risk, if necessary, to do what perhaps has never been done before to help a customer. Not only will you likely have that customer coming back, but in the process, he or she might in turn share the positive experience with others.

Be the person others look to, take on challenges, and get things done. Jump on opportunities, offer a helping hand or a timely suggestion, make a plan, and work your plan. Seek help and recruit others as needed to get the job done. Volunteer, follow through, and finish what you commit to doing.

Often, a project, assignment, or responsibility can initially seem next to impossible, but as you dig in and explore possibilities, you can be surprised by what you can achieve.

Some employees (and companies) find their greatest success when going after a seemingly impossible challenge. At Johnsville Foods, management was going to decline a customer order because it would require a record level of production within a short time period. Instead, they presented the request to all employees and various teams worked on possible solutions until a plan was devised to make the deadline. A new production record was set in less time than was even anticipated as the entire organization pulled together to meet the challenge.

When the office of Amy's Ice Cream in Austin, Texas, happened to run out of job application forms, a quick-thinking employee handed each remaining applicant an empty bag with instructions to do something creative with it. This brainstorm allowed applicants to demonstrate their ability to be creative and entertain others—important job attributes to the company. The bags quickly became a standard part of the interview process.

Nothing ever can be achieved when you focus only on why it can't be done—you need to focus instead on what can be done and how you can be the one to do it. Brainstorm. Try different combinations and strategies for "thinking outside of the box." Use a "fish bone" problem-solving technique to think through a plan in which various problems and solutions can be addressed.

Post a flip chart page on a wall in the lunchroom with a stated problem on top of the sheet and ask for ideas and solutions from whomever is interested in responding.

☞ LOOK FOR THE POSITIVE IN PROBLEMS

Every problem has a positive side and provides an opportunity to shine.

If you encounter a problem in your job, don't immediately view it as negative or refer it to your manager or others to resolve. Instead, determine the impact of the problem. Consider why the problem arose and if it is a recurring problem. Examine the circumstances that led to the problem and how those circumstances are changing over time. Project into the future the likelihood of the problem getting worse or better. Then think of how you can turn the situation into a positive opportunity.

When Machinery Services Corporation in Paterson, New Jersey, ran out of stainless-steel U-bolts, one employee of their supplier, Fastenal, in Hackensack, New Jersey, thought this was great news because it gave him a chance to rise to the occasion. Keith Greaves drove to the hub in Scranton, Pennsylvania, at 2 A.M. to personally deliver the needed U-bolts by 6:30 A.M. The customer was delighted, which in turn led to additional business.

The customer has remained very loyal to the supplier ever since.

When a government agency in New Zealand printed a number of brochures with an incorrect toll-free phone number and distributed them throughout the country, the result was a flood of confused calls to CLEAR Communications, the owner of the incorrect phone number. A bright sales agent struck on a way to make the problem an opportunity and called the government agency and sold them the incorrect phone number, not only solving the problem for both organizations but also generating a sale from someone else's mistake.

When Rhino Foods, a Burlington, Vermont–based supplier of chocolate-chip cookie dough to Ben & Jerry's, experienced a downturn in business a few years ago, some 25 percent of the workforce was scheduled to be laid off. A team of employees volunteered to try to find ways to avert this crisis. The group came up with a plan that sought employee volunteers to work as paid employees at local firms that needed temporary help.

The company agreed to maintain the volunteers' seniority and benefits as well

as make up the difference for those employees who had to take a pay cut in
their temporary jobs. No one was subse-
quently laid off, and human resource director Marlene Dailey said the action
"was really effective during a potentially
devastating time . . . it ended up cement-
ing the team."

Look for the positive in negative solutions. Step back from the situation or
take a long-term view to gain perspec-
tive. Brainstorm alternative solutions
and evaluate each to determine the best
course of action and decide what part of
that solution you could implement.

☞ BE A PERSON WHO MAKES THINGS HAPPEN

Be a person of action! Don't overanalyze situations, rather size things up quickly and act. Doing so will help you achieve more and develop your skill and judgment for future actions.

When Gail Seto was being hired as an assistant manager at the Gap in Toronto, Ontario, she noticed that the company's standard policy and procedures manual didn't cover half the issues that come up in a typical store. On her own initiative, Gail drafted a concise training handbook to use as a quick guide to running a Gap store, which was eventually adapted for Gap stores throughout Canada. From then on, management turned to Gail for other tasks, and before long she was promoted.

Kathleen Betts, a mother of two who shared her job working for the Massachusetts state government with another mom, was concerned about a pending layoff. Using only her personal time away from the office, Betts researched the state's Medicaid rules and Federal

Department of Human Services guidelines and uncovered an accounting wrinkle that entitled the state to get reimbursed at a much higher rate than it had been, providing the state a $489 million windfall. Betts received a cash award of $10,000 for her initiative and work, as well as thanks from a very grateful governor.

One employee describes her role as someone who takes initiative in the following way: "As a change agent, I am committed to change within myself and my organization and my society. This means that I try to think about the long-term ramifications of the actions and policies of others and myself. I lobby for win-win situations. My organization sees me as someone who can be counted on to speak up, ask questions, and make suggestions. This is not part of my official job description."

Take the initiative. Do not assume that management must know about and must be doing something to fix a bad situation. Seldom will this be the case; and as change continues to escalate in all aspects of business, management will be even less likely to know what is needed. To wait for management's attention, therefore, is to court disaster and risk losing the customer, your job, or even the business itself.

TAKE RESPONSIBILITY FOR YOUR
ACTIONS (AND INACTIONS)

Take responsibility for yourself, for your actions, and, yes, for your *in*actions. Hold yourself accountable to your own standard—and have that be a *higher* standard than that of those around you. Take your obligations seriously and yourself lightly. Own up to your mistakes when you make them and focus on what you learned from those mistakes.

Look in the mirror and ask yourself: "Did I do what I said I would do when I said I would do it?" "Did I listen to my colleagues?" "Did I get all the facts, pro and con?" "Was I open to suggestions?" "Did I do my best work possible?"

Do things without having to be reminded, and be your own worst critic in evaluating what you have done. Proof your work.

For example, before an assignment is due, provide your boss an interim status report and tentative recommendations to gauge his or her reactions and concerns. Having your final effort include responses to that feedback will increase your chances of success.

Be a person of your word and hold yourself accountable for following through on your commitments. If you change the agreed-upon commitment or plan, check to see if that is okay with those you committed to.

Persevere—Don't Give Up Easily

After you have identified ideas and opportunities to make a difference, and have researched the best strategies and taken appropriate action, you still may meet with some obstacles. How you handle these obstacles can in large part determine your ultimate success and make the difference between someone who just brings up problems and ideas and someone who is able to make things happen to resolve problems and act on ideas and opportunities.

Those who take initiative have a belief and passion in their idea that drives them ever forward, regardless of setbacks or obstacles, to make their idea happen. They never, ever give up on something they truly believe in.

☞ REGROUP WHEN YOUR IDEAS MEET RESISTANCE

Don't be swayed when an idea you have hits a snag or meets with resistance. Instead, stop, reassess your options, and find some other way to push forward on an idea in which you believe.

Dina Campion, an employee of Starbucks in Santa Monica, California, pushed an icy coffee drink she thought customers would like. Dubbed the "Frappuccino," the drink was not authorized by corporate, and she was told not to sell it in the Starbucks where she worked.

Undeterred, she kept selling the drink to customers and turned in a sales report for the month showing it to be one of the more popular coffee drinks with their customers.

She then received a call from Howard Schultz, CEO of Starbucks, thanking her for ignoring his edict. The Frappuccino became a national hit and earned the company $100 million in its first year alone.

Granted, you don't want to make a habit of blatantly disobeying management's wishes, but in some instances, if you truly believe that a certain course of action would make the company better or more successful, it may make sense to pursue your belief knowing you risk being reprimanded or even possibly losing your job.

If an idea bogs down, reassess the situation. Focus on new possibilities. Be positive. Bounce the idea off additional colleagues and get their help in thinking it through. Do check your homework to determine what additional resources would be needed to implement your idea and the savings potential to the organization if the idea were implemented. Represent your idea with a revised plan for implementing it.

☞ DON'T TRUST YOUR MANAGER'S OPEN DOOR

Be respectful of your manager's time and don't abuse your access to him or her.

Most managers today know it's expected that they be open and encouraging to their employees, even when they don't feel like doing so. Be the employee who is savvy about selecting the best time to have impact with your manager and preparing well for the time you both do meet.

Josiah, a housing-mortgage specialist at a Fortune 500 bank, wanted to initiate a flextime schedule where he worked, but even though management listened to his idea, it wasn't interested in pursuing it. When a new CEO came aboard, Josiah took the opportunity to propose a flextime program. The new CEO agreed to it, and soon after, many of the department's workers shifted their work schedules, and productivity soared.

Choosing the right time to act can even include picking the best time of the day or of the week to put forth an idea or ask for permission about an action you want to take. For example, if your manager has a habit of making phone calls and answering e-mail in the mornings, don't interrupt her to talk about an idea you have. Instead, respect her routine and ask when the best time to talk might be.

Your manager has enough to do—she doesn't need you to bring her additional work. If you have a problem, first try to solve it yourself. If you need to involve your manager, respect her time, as you would want your own time to be respected. In dealing with your manager, always put forth recommendations for action, alternative solutions, or a plan for resolution.

The hallmark of getting things done is a relentless focus on closure, that is, overcoming the odds and obstacles that stop most people in their tracks.

Madelon Kuhn, an employee at 1-800-FLOWERS, headquartered in Westbury, New York, demonstrates persistence when she refuses to be stymied by difficult flower orders. On one such occasion, an order for flowers was to be sent to Johnston Island in Hawaii. The only problem was that no one had ever heard of the island, let alone tried to send an order there.

Madelon, however, took the assignment one step at a time and identified the specific location (the Christmas Islands) after calling the Air Force (she only had a post office address). She then evaluated options to deliver flowers and was finally able to have a florist drop off the order to Air Macedonia for a trip to the island.

Hewlett-Packard engineer Charles House was given a medal for "extraordinary contempt and defiance beyond the normal call of engineering duty" because he ignored an order from company founder David Packard to stop working on a type of high-quality video monitor. Despite the rebuke, House pressed ahead and succeeded in developing the monitor, which has been used in heart transplants and in tracking NASA's manned moon landings.

Be the person who overcomes obstacles and rises to meet challenges instead of shying away from adversity. If the cost has made an action prohibitive, look for ways to achieve the goal without a budget or alternative sources of funding. If someone has a reputation for being difficult to work with, be determined to win that individual over and have the best of working relationships. If the team you're part of feels there is no way to meet an important deadline, focus on what would need to happen in order to meet the deadline, not why it will never be met.

If one approach does not work, keep to your goal, but try something different.

For example, I work to help managers and companies improve the ways they recognize and help motivate their employees. One challenge that frequently arises is how to persuade top management to support a recognition initiative.

The answer to this challenge varies depending upon many factors, foremost of which is how those top managers are best persuaded. If they need research or best practices, provide that. If they want a cost-benefit analysis, do that. If an internal pilot project has been helpful to demonstrate an idea was viable, consider doing a pilot program (and pick one that will likely show positive, desired results!).

Look at other successful initiatives that have occurred in the company's past and evaluate the process for how they were approved and completed. Was a task force created to recommend solutions to a pressing problem? Was funding taken from other budget items? Was the project linked to an existing initiative that was expanded? Did the initiative have an executive sponsor? Other initiatives can serve as a prototype for success of your idea as well.

People are persuaded differently, so your approach to winning them over must also vary. One technique or approach is not likely to work in all circumstances, and the more approaches you have to reach your goal, the more likely you will do so.

I've seen projects that were initially unsupported become fast-tracked when linked to a pressing issue or corporate value, for example, or when there was a personal presentation (and appeal) to the head of a division or the president of the company.

If, at first, an idea that you feel has merit is not accepted, wait for a better time and a different set of circumstances to make it happen. In the meantime, further develop the details and support for implementing the change, look to what other companies are doing, and prepare for a more successful time.

☞ LEARN TO ENJOY THOSE THINGS
THAT OTHERS HATE TO DO

To be good at and enjoy doing things that others hate to do will give you many opportunities to be a hero at work.

This can range from taking minutes at staff meetings to making presentations to dealing with a difficult customer. All will add value to your contribution in the work group and will help you gain both the appreciation of your colleagues and the respect of those above you in the organization.

Taking notes for the group in a meeting is a good example. Few people seem to like to take minutes in a meeting, yet this responsibility is important to helping the group get its work done and thus is a useful task to take on. It also provides an opportunity to expand on items of special interest to you and to help shape the follow-up actions that are needed.

Reviewing applications is another task that seems to be dull yet can give you the inside track on potential hires. If you work in sales, come to love cold-calling or to be prompt with paperwork.

For anyone, a well-organized work station will always be an asset.

Look to the person to whom you report and ask to take over the tasks he or she hates doing. You might likewise want to be interested in budgeting, purchasing, special task forces, and other opportunities that give you the potential to both learn and grow, as well as to gain visibility in the organization.

CAUTION

AVOID THE "BLAME GAME"

Most employees do only what is specifically requested of them. They are quick to defer to their manager or to a policy when a problem arises.

If they are ever challenged on an action, they are experts at playing "the blame game," that is, blaming everybody and everything around them for the problem—sometimes even the customer. Not only does this not help the situation, the negative energy generated makes the situation worse.

Instead, try asking yourself: "What could I have done to prevent this problem?" "What can we learn from this situation?" and "How can we improve things together going forward?"

Be positive when faced with negative situations and negative people. Be a role model. Look to the future and decide upon the best course of action given the existing circumstances.

Excuses are the first defense of the insecure. Blaming circumstances often leads to blaming others. Catch yourself when you find you are making an excuse and stop. Turn your focus instead to what can be done to best rectify the situation as soon as possible. Be positive and forward-looking.

Part Four

COMMON
CONCERNS

What Holds Us Back

Doing what needs to be done without waiting to be told involves taking risks. Most people, I've learned, are risk-averse, preferring to play it safe. I find we tend not to take initiative because of *fear, frustration,* or *failure.* The following discussion offers some thoughts for overcoming each of these concerns.

Fear

☞ **"I MIGHT MAKE A MISTAKE."**

I can only hope that you will! Many, in fact! You can learn a lot from your mistakes, and if you never have any, you may just have a lot you still need to learn. Mistakes can help you become stronger, and thus able to do more.

Sure, no one likes to look wrong or feel stupid, but people who are up front about their intentions are rarely faulted if those intentions are good or in the best interests of the organization.

What is the risk of trying something new? Some time, some effort, some obstacles, and possibly some rejection. What is the risk of not trying? A loss of potential—for the situation, for yourself, and for the organization.

Face your fears. Ask yourself what is the worst that could possibly happen, then act to minimize that possibility.

Everyone has fears of failure, but successful people learn to transfer their fears into actions that will enhance their chances of success. We all have to stretch in order to grow, and if your fear of making mistakes keeps you from trying, learning, and growing, you will ultimately lose out anyway.

You always have the ability to focus on what you learned from a mistake, and typically, there is some positive in even the worst of situations.

☞ "WHAT NEEDS TO BE DONE IS NOT EASY."

If something was easy to do, it most likely would have been done some time ago by somebody else. Expect to be met with resistance and you won't be disappointed. Few new ideas are met with open enthusiasm. After all, if it's such a great idea, why didn't we do it two years ago?

Strive to make your idea doable. Do something different to move in the desired direction. Assess what seems to work better, what seems to work worse, and what seems to make no difference at all. Do more of what seems to work. Leverage your successes to make greater progress on your journey.

Remember, too, that you don't have to do things all at once. You can have an idea, talk about the idea with others, make a list, pursue some exploratory items, and build up to a simple proposal to management. In other words, make the difficult easier by dividing it into smaller, doable tasks.

No one wants to be fired, of course, but there are worse things that can happen to you (although you may not think so at the time!).

What can be more scary than being fired, however, is the possibility that you may lose control of your life and feel stuck in a job you hate. Be more afraid of not being alive, of being complacent, and of living your life on someone else's terms.

I have a friend who, in his first career job, saved until he had enough money to cover three months' worth of expenses just so he would have the security to be able to walk away from any job that wasn't working for him.

There's false security that occurs when we become comfortable with a paycheck. If you're not constantly learning, growing, and pushing to do your best, a job loss is likely in your future anyway.

If you've developed your skills and marketability in your current job, finding another job when, and if, you need to is a lot less painful than the fear that paralyzes you from taking risks.

The best defense against having others be dissatisfied with your work is to be proactive in making sure what you do is relevant and important to the needs of your manager, the department, and the organization.

Frustration

☞ "I DON'T HAVE THE AUTHORITY."

Seldom is anyone given enough authority to take the actions necessary to improve things in their job all by themselves. The best authority today is not the formal authority of position, but rather the authority that is earned from one's past successes and one's ability to influence others to get things done.

Authority is better assumed than it is granted. As you assume authority to pursue the best interests of the organization, you will be granted greater leeway to take even greater initiative.

You can assume authority at different levels, with increasing degrees of risk: You can seek permission in advance, you can act and then seek permission, or you can act and not seek permission. Of course, keeping your manager informed is always going to be the best policy. No one likes unpleasant surprises.

The more authority you assume and

manage well for the good of the organization, the easier it will be for you to gain approval for upcoming actions you advocate. The more you do, the more you will be able to do.

☞ "I DON'T HAVE THE SUPPORT."

It's rare to have a manager who openly backs everything you want to do. You have to gain your manager's support over time through your actions.

Perhaps your manager has chastised you in the past when you've taken initiative. Although this can leave anybody feeling burned and unsupported, do not despair. Help your manager see the value of what you want to do. Give your manager confidence that you can get results through your plan, preparation, and persistence, and in the process, help him or her and the department look good as well.

Build your support with others in the organization, ideally within existing systems, processes, and procedures.

It may seem difficult to act to improve things at work if your manager is "micromanaging you," that is, constantly focusing on the details of your job and leaving you little latitude for independent thought or action. To change this scenario, first try to understand why your manager is like this. Does he or she manage everyone in this way? Is it a function of the task or the mood your manager is in? Talk with him or her about improving the situation and allowing you more room to operate.

Often employees don't realize that their manager's actions are in response to their own previous actions. After all, if you've never shown initiative to do things right, can you really expect your manager to trust that you'll do them at all?

☞ "I DON'T HAVE THE SKILLS."

Most skills are developed in your current job responsibilities. These skills range from personal effectiveness and interpersonal skills to technical expertise and your ability to work well with others as part of a team. Make plans to systematically develop the skills you need to be successful over time.

Investigate what programs if any are available to you in your organization: languages, computer skills, and so on. If none are available, research and see if you can get approval to take a class or seminar that can help you better do your job.

You will never have these skills if you never seek to develop them. As with most things, the more you do, the easier it becomes. Bring an element of experimentation to your job. In addition to exploring new and likely better ways to get things done, your time will be more exciting.

Failure

☞ **"I TOOK INITIATIVE ONCE AND MADE A MISTAKE."**

It's often difficult to see the strength in failure—especially at the time—but failure can indeed make you stronger if you learn from it.

By learning, I don't mean telling yourself: "I'll never get in that situation again!" Rather, ask yourself a few questions: "How would I do it differently next time?" "Who would I involve?" "What other approach might have helped me overcome the obstacles I faced?"

It's okay to make mistakes. The key is to learn from them. Take some time to think about what went wrong and ask (yourself and others) what you could have done differently to prevent the error. Have a plan should the same situation or circumstances arise again.

When discussing the problem with others, be open to their feedback and suggestions. Accept feedback as a gift and thank others for offering it to you.

You don't have to do everything that others suggest, but having someone else help evaluate and think through your actions will always be an asset for you.

As the saying goes: "Nothing ventured, nothing gained." The nature of any type of initiative involves risk and the possibility of failure. If you never make any mistakes, chances are you won't be learning or growing, and you won't likely achieve much, either.

☞ "SOMEONE KEEPS BLOCKING MY EFFORTS"

The more aggressive you are about your ideas, the more likely it is that others will have objections to what you want to do and how and when you want to do it. You may be a threat to them or they may feel your success will make them look bad. Remember, too, that criticism from others is often well intended, as others are trying to help you think through your plans and avoid mistakes.

From time to time, you will have to deal with another person at work who is difficult, who blocks your efforts at every turn. It's not always easy to know why people choose to be like this, but you should give them the benefit of the doubt that they believe in what they are doing and the reasons that they oppose you.

Talk to your perceived enemies. Get to know them. Tell them you appreciate what they do for you. Ask them how you can be of help to them. See what you can do to incorporate their suggestions and minimize the concerns they have for your plans.

If you make the first step and go most

of the distance to make the relationship work, most people will be willing to meet you the rest of the way. Once they feel you understand them and are on their side, it is easier to gain their confidence and support.

Of course, some people come to hate their jobs and—as a consequence—strive to make everyone else's job miserable as well. Still, it will serve you best to take the high road and treat these people with the trust and respect you would like them to afford you.

☞ "I CONSTANTLY FAIL WHEN I TRY TO TAKE INITIATIVE."

Some people are not good at taking initiative. They don't like taking initiative, they feel it's not their job to take initiative, and they are unsuccessful more often than not when they attempt to do so.

If you are one of these individuals, you need to assess the situation and either find a job in which you can be successful just doing what you are told, or seek a more drastic approach to breaking out of your past behavioral patterns.

Some people prefer to have a job in which they are told what to do—you might be one of them. If so, you need to select a highly structured, highly routine work environment and a manager who holds more traditional views about the way work should be done. Unfortunately, given your safe outlook on life, you may have limitations on your career opportunities.

Another approach would be to stop playing it safe and dramatically reinvent yourself to become a "take charge" kind of person. You might enroll in a Dale Carnegie course, join a Toastmasters Club, or consider increasing your networking opportunities through professional associations.

At some point you also need to ask yourself, "Am I in the right job, working for the right company?" If you are constantly at odds with the expectations and responsibilities of your position, it may mean you're doing the wrong job, or are in the wrong company.

You should consider finding a work environment that best supports who you are, and the values, skills, and aptitudes you bring to your job. A more supportive work environment is a great foundation upon which to build.

Part Five

IN
CONCLUSION—
THE ULTIMATE
REWARD

Realize Your Potential

I always believed that if I worked hard and did what I was told, I would be successful in life. But as a cashier in a 7-Eleven in my youth, I learned this attitude was not enough. To be successful and get the most out of life, we each have to assert ourselves to make a difference.

Now I believe the biggest mistake in life is to think you work for somebody else. Here is what I try to remind myself every day.

We all ultimately work for ourselves. Sure, others might sign your paycheck. They might assign you work and evaluate your performance. But more important, you drive your own boat. You are the sole determinant of your ideas and actions.

Talk about your ideas with others. Volunteer with activities that will take you closer to your passion. Determine what you are good at, as well as what you enjoy. Get yourself into a work environment that supports who you are and what you want to be. Work on your strengths more than your weaknesses so you can maximize your talents.

We all have a store of untapped energy. Most of us are waiting for someone else to recognize this and, with it, our potential. We are waiting for others to—in one way or another—tell us what to do and when to do it.

We go through life bouncing from one job to another, seldom happy with anything that we do and uncertain about what we should do to improve things.

Day after day, we repeat a routine that seems secure only in that we have done it so many times before. At home, we read the paper and watch television. At work, we go through the motions, often playing it safe as much as possible.

We are waiting for a wake-up call, but we never set the alarm.

The average employee ranks three out of every four managers they've had in their careers as poor. Most of us hope to be lucky and get that one "good" manager out of four who makes our jobs, our careers—and our lives—more worthwhile.

If you want to change your life, it has

to start with you. Take control. Be responsible for your actions. Avoid excuses, and instead find ways to make those things happen that are important to you and your employer. Surround yourself with like-minded people who also are energized and looking to make the most out of their lives.

Avoid people who either don't understand what is important to you or are not interested in being a part of your dream. Gravitate to those individuals who support and encourage you, whom you can look up to and aspire to be like.

Be a person who makes things happen—starting with yourself. Adopt the slogan "If it's to be, it needs to begin with me."

Your thoughts shape your beliefs about yourself and your reality and, in very real and direct ways, affect your actions.

Don't wait for others to tell you what to do. See for yourself what needs to be done! Listen. Learn. Take a stand. Make a suggestion. Volunteer to take action. Most important, do what you say you will do. Not the fifth time, not the second time—but the first time. Be a person of your word who can be relied upon to follow through without a series of reminders and constant badgering. Be one step ahead of identifying the needs of those around you—your manager, your co-workers, your customers—and act on that information.

Bring solutions to your manager, not problems. And with those solutions, bring energy for putting them into action.

Life passes so many people by when, at any time, they can get on board. Work on improving your current job, not the next one. Do it now, not when you feel you eventually will have time.

Live your dreams, don't postpone them. Find any way to identify and grab hold of your purpose. Find the spark that lights your enthusiasm, then fan it into a flame of passion. Doing so will make you invaluable not only to your employer—but to yourself.

Lead with your initiative. Take on the challenge to strive to be your best and then determine how you can do just that. Action speaks louder than words, and inaction says nothing at all.

When all is said and done, more is

said and little is done. Be the exception to this rule. Be the person known for action and for taking initiative. Not only will you develop a skill that is in high demand, but your life will become more worth living.

The risk you face is not in taking chances and trying to do things that have never been done, but in *not* doing them and never knowing if you could have done them. The risk is in being just an average employee: someone who simply shows up and does what he or she is told to do.

You can't afford to be just average—and your employer can't afford to have you be only average!

Be on fire. Have a passion for what you are doing with your life that is impossible to put out. Think constantly about how you can achieve what you're after. Fill your days with actions that make a difference, all linked by a common passion. Pick up energy with each passing hour of the day.

Rather than being shaped by your circumstances, realize that you have control over them. You can make things happen that will improve your situation.

You can be in charge of your own destiny. Your future is in your own hands. Shape your future by remembering these simple words:

DON'T JUST DO WHAT YOU ARE TOLD, DO WHAT NEEDS TO BE DONE.

What I Tell You	What Needs to Be Done
Include a note with materials sent	Draft and type the note, let me review it
Send a customer a package	Follow up to make sure it arrived
Follow up on a potential lead	Sell the client; let me know the outcome
Turn off the lights when you leave	Don't waste money or electricity
Ask people what they think	Categorize what they say, make recommendations
Send a contract	Follow up on issues raised, bring to closure
Deal with an upset customer	Resolve the problem, make the customer happy
Check on a problem	Fix the problem, revise the system to avoid recurrence
Develop a proposal	Research options, get buy-in by those affected
Check on a price	Do comparisons, make a recommendation
Select a supplier	Create criteria and selection process, get bids
Two employees are at odds	Mediate and help broker better communication
Create a list of past due accounts	Find ways to improve cash flow
Our overhead is increasing	Help us to reduce costs
Sales are down	Find ways to increase revenues and help close sales

ABOUT THE AUTHOR

Bob Nelson, Ph.D., is president of Nelson Motivation Inc. in San Diego, California, and author of the bestselling books *1001 Ways to Reward Employees, 1001 Ways to Energize Employees, 1001 Ways to Take Initiative at Work,* and *Managing for Dummies.*

For additional information, products, or services, contact Nelson Motivation Inc. at 1-800-575-5521 or (outside the U.S.) at 1-858-487-1046, or visit www.nelson-motivation.com. You can also contact Bob Nelson directly via the Internet at BobRewards@aol.com.